MYSTERIES OF THE PAST

SHIPWRECKS

Jason Hook

RAINTREE
STECK-VAUGHN
PUBLISHERS

A Harcourt Company

Austin   New York
www.raintreesteckvaughn.com

LOOK FOR THE SHIPWRECK BOX

Look for the little black shipwreck in boxes like this. Here you will find extra facts, stories, and other interesting information about shipwrecks.

Published by Raintree Steck-Vaughn, an imprint of Steck-Vaughn Company.

Library of Congress Cataloging-in-Publication Data

Hook, Jason.
  Shipwrecks / Jason Hook
    p.cm. -- (Mysteries of the past)
  Includes bibliographical references (p.)
  ISBN 0-7398-4340-0
    1. Shipwrecks--Juvenile literature.
  [1. Shipwrecks.] I. Title. II. Mysteries of the Past

G525 .H813 2001
910.4'52--dc21   2001019051

Printed in Hong Kong / China
1 2 3 4 5 6 7 8 9 05 04 03 02 01

Acknowledgments
We wish to thank the following individuals and organizations for their help and assistance and for supplying material in their collections: AKG London 5 top, 9 bottom (John Hios); Ancient Art and Architecture Collection 9 top; Art Archive 4 (Dagli Orti), 11 top (Magdalene College, Cambridge/ Eileen Tweedie), 12 (Eileen Tweedie), 14 (Cornelis de Vries), 16 top (Naval Museum, Genoa/Dagli Orti), 18 top (Eileen Tweedie), 26 (Musée du Louvre, Paris/Josse); Corbis 1 (Ralph White), 3 bottom (Ralph White), 10 (Adam Wolfitt), 15 top (Macduff Everton), 23 top and bottom (Ralph White), 25 (Bettmann), 27 (Hulton-Deutsch), 30 (Adam Wolfitt); CM Dixon 8; Institute of Nautical Archaeology 3 top, 6, 7; Kobal Collection 16 bottom; Mary Evans Picture Library 19, 20 right, 29 bottom; National Maritime Museum, London 13 bottom; Old Dartmouth Historical Society, New Bedford Whaling Museum 17, 29 top; Peter Newark's Pictures 2, 18 bottom, 20 left, 21, 22, 24 top and bottom; Rex Features 28, 31; Topham Picturepoint 11 bottom, 15 bottom; Ulster Museum 13 top.

► (Top) Treasure from the world's oldest shipwreck in Turkey. (See page 6.)

► (Bottom) Survivors from the famous ship, the *Titanic*, that sank in 1912. (See page 22.)

◄ A poster used to sell trips on the ship *Lusitania*, which was sunk by a German torpedo. (See page 24.)

CONTENTS

SHIPWRECKS

The wrecks of hundreds of ships deep in the ocean, lie half-buried by sand. In the dark, thousands of feet under the ocean, the ships look like great piles of bones. Just think how many mysteries they must hold!

▼ The first sailors had nothing like this map of the African coast. This was drawn in 1570.

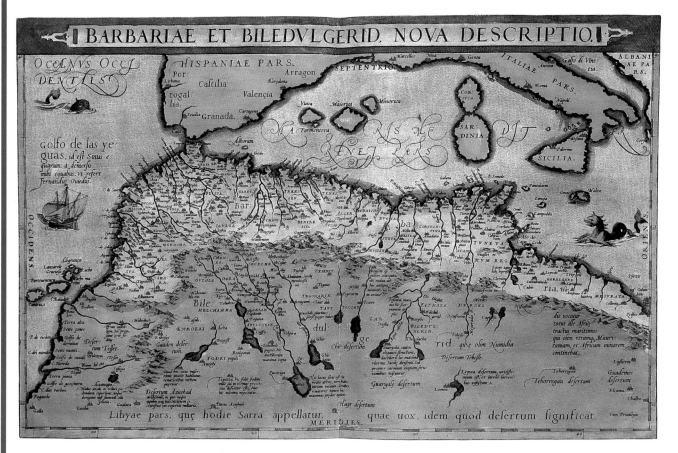

People have sailed across the oceans since the ancient Egyptians first sailed the seas 5,000 years ago. These first sailors had no tools or maps to help them avoid rocks and other dangers. So very often they were shipwrecked.

▲ In early times,
many people believed
that shipwrecks were
caused by sea
monsters.

Ships are wrecked on reefs, or ridges of coral, and rocks by storms. They can hit icebergs, whales, or each other. They can also be wrecked by pirates, sailors, wars, and fire.

We can tell a lot about the sailors on these wrecked ships by what we find on the wrecks. They hold the tools, clothes, weapons, and treasures from long ago that tell us what life was like for the men on board.

First, we raise a shipwreck and the things it carried with it—its ancient cargo. Then we can uncover the clues to help solve the mysteries that are hidden inside a shipwreck.

 THE FIRST WRECK

The oldest story of a shipwreck comes from an Egyptian sailor whose ship sunk in the Red Sea in the Middle East nearly 4,000 years ago. He writes, "We flew before the wind... the ship went down; of all in it only I survived." The sailor then claims he was saved by a 49-foot-(15-m-) long monster!

ANCIENT TREASURE

Over 3,000 years ago, a ship sailed past the coast of Ulu Burun in Turkey. On board was an amazing cargo: hundreds of blocks of copper; jars big enough to hide a human; golden jewelry; wine, oil, and perfume; fruit and ostrich eggs; elephant tusks and hippopotamus teeth.

The ship was carrying such a heavy load that, when a terrible storm blew up, it sunk beneath the waves. This ship took its treasures down with it.

The ship lay on the ocean floor until 1982, when a diver saw what looked like metal cakes with ears on the seabed. When they were carefully uncovered, explorers found that these "cakes" were blocks of copper with handles. Underneath them was the oldest shipwreck ever found.

Beautiful gold jewelry like this small statue and ring were found on the Ulu Burun shipwreck.

 QUEEN OF EGYPT

In the ship's cargo was a golden jewel, a scarab. The word "Nefertiti" was on it. This was the name of an Egyptian queen who lived 3,500 years ago. Egyptian paintings from this time show Syrian trading ships. These paintings tell us what the Ulu Burun ship might have looked like.

Mud had kept the ship's goods from falling to pieces. The ship probably traded along the coasts of Syria, Palestine, Egypt, Greece, and Turkey. A trader's weights were also found on board. These may have been used for weighing gold or other goods. The trader must have been very upset by the loss of his cargo—if he survived!

◀▲ Over 3,000 years ago, sailors at Ulu Burun wore the gold jewelry shown here.

▼ At the Ulu Burun shipwreck, divers found many ancient jars that had once held precious goods.

GREEN WOMEN

A man was diving in the seas along the coast of the Greek island of Antikythera in October 1900. He had been diving for sponges, but instead he saw what looked like a heap of dead green women lying at the bottom of the sea. What had the diver found?

▼ This statue of a boy was found at the Antikythera shipwreck.

A second diver quickly worked out the mystery. The "green women" were bronze statues that had changed color in the seawater over time. They were part of the cargo from an ancient shipwreck. It lay under 197 feet (60 m) of water—deep enough to make diving very dangerous. But one by one, a team of divers brought the statues to the surface. They were of a bearded teacher, a sportsman, a young boy, and a huge bull.

COMPUTER AGE

Divers found another mystery on the Antikythera shipwreck. It was a bronze machine with all kinds of wheels on it. Scientists studied the inside of this strange object. They learned that it was an ancient "computer." It had once been used to work out the movements of the Sun and Moon!

This bronze head of a teacher was found on the seabed.

This picture shows the parts of the bronze "computer" found at Antikythera. In the background you can see a model of the ship.

Modern studies of the wood in the Antikythera ship have shown that it was built in Italy about 2,100 years ago. It probably belonged to a Roman trader or soldier. The Greek statues carried on the ship may have been traded or stolen, but they never made it to Italy anyway.

9

HENRY'S WARSHIP

King Henry VIII watched from the land when French ships attacked British ships on Sunday, July 19, 1545. The *Mary Rose*, one of Henry's finest warships, sailed out to join the battle. Suddenly, the wind rocked the ship, and it turned over and sank.

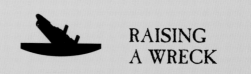

RAISING A WRECK

Over 24,000 dives were made to study the *Mary Rose*. In 1982, the ship was raised, and it is now shown in Portsmouth, England. To stop the hull from cracking, the workers need to spray the wood with a special chemical all of the time, for the next 20 years.

◄ Lions' heads decorate this bronze cannon from the wreck of the *Mary Rose*.

The *Mary Rose* sank into the seabed, where it stayed for over 430 years. Then, in 1982, archaeologists used a huge metal cradle to lift the ship. They found all kinds of things, including meat-bones, peas, and plums; leather shoes and knee-high boots; and chessboards. These things tell us a lot about what sailors ate, how they dressed, and what games they played in the 1500s.

10

▼ This is the only picture that we have of the *Mary Rose* from the time when Henry VIII was king.

But why did the *Mary Rose* sink? The wreck also helped scientists to work out this mystery. She was carrying heavy guns, called cannons, that were fired through hatches in the side of the ship. When the wind rocked the ship, the weight of these cannons must have tipped it over. Water poured into the ship, and the *Mary Rose* sank with over 600 men on board.

▼ The *Mary Rose* is on show in Portsmouth, England.

ARMADA GOLD

Strong winds blew the *Girona* around as her captain looked for a safe place to hide from the storm. The *Girona* was one of many ships caught in the terrible weather that day. These ships were part of the Spanish Armada that had tried to attack England. But they had failed, and now they were trying to get back home to Spain.

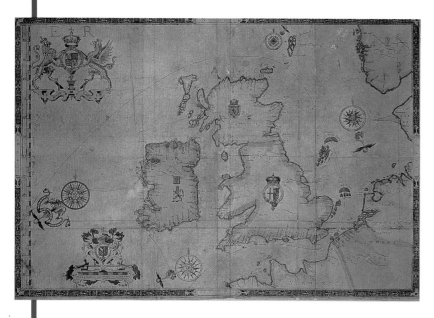

◀ This map shows how the Armada traveled around England, Scotland, and the north of Ireland.

The strong winds of 1588 wrecked 20 of the Armada's ships on Ireland's rocky coast. The *Girona* was one of them, but for years nobody knew where the wreck lay.

A Belgian diver named Robert Stenuit spent months studying old maps, until he found a bay named Spanish Point. He dove there in 1967 and found the Spanish wreck that the bay was named for.

SHATTERED BY STORMS

Only about 70 of the Armada's 130 ships made it home to Spain. About 30 ships were lost during the battle, and 30 more were shipwrecked on the coasts of Ireland and Scotland. Those ships were blown onto rocks by the terrible storms. As many as 15,000 Spanish sailors and soldiers died.

But Stenuit found another mystery. The *Girona* was carrying too much treasure!

There were chains, rings, gold buttons, and coins from six countries. Stenuit found out that the *Girona* had rescued survivors from two other shipwrecks. When it sunk, the ship was carrying 1,300 Spanish sailors, the crew of three ships, and all their treasures!

◀ This treasure was found on the shipwreck of the *Girona*.

▼ Spanish and English ships battle in the sea, off the coast of England.

THE DEADLY CARVINGS

For 333 years the wreck of the Swedish warship *Vasa* lay under 98 feet (30 m) of water just outside Stockholm Harbor, Sweden. In 1961 archaeologists put thick ropes under the oak hull, and two ships brought it slowly to the ocean surface.

Divers found 700 beautiful wooden carvings of knights, emperors, lions, monsters, and mermaids lying around the wreck. These beautiful painted figures had once decorated the *Vasa*. They had fallen away from the ship's cabin walls when the nails that kept them up rotted away in the seawater.

▲ A modern artist painted this picture of the *Vasa*.

DIVING BELLS

In the 1660s, Swedish diver Albrecht von Treileben rescued bronze cannons from the *Vasa*. He used an early form of diving bell, a tank with an open bottom. He stood on a platform under the bell, with most of his body in the water. Air inside the bell kept his head dry and allowed him to breathe.

▲ This picture shows the *Vasa*'s beautiful carvings.

◄ The *Vasa* has had a lot of work done on it. It is now on display in Stockholm, Sweden.

The carvings explained how the *Vasa* sank. On August 10, 1628, it had set out on the first journey. Flags flew from the masts and the sun shone on the carvings. Crowds cheered as it sailed away. But the *Vasa* never even left the harbor. The heavy carvings upset the ship's balance. A gust of wind caught the *Vasa*'s sails, and it tipped over. The ship with the beautiful carvings sank from sight.

SUNK BY A WHALE

The scary tale of the shipwrecked *Essex* was as famous in the 1800s as the story of the *Titanic* is today. The *Essex* was used by American sailors to hunt whales. The wreck has never been raised, but reports written by the eight people who survived the sinking, tell of a terrible mystery.

◀ This picture was painted in the 1800s and shows sailors on a whaling ship after they have killed a whale.

On November 20, 1820, the *Essex* was hunting whales in the Pacific. Suddenly, a 98 foot- (30 m-) long sperm whale swam up from the depths of the sea and moved toward the ship. Twice it hit the *Essex* with its giant head. It must have felt like they had hit a rock. With the sides of the ship crushed, the *Essex* quickly sank.

▲ This is a picture from the film that was made of the book *Moby Dick*. (See next page.)

Twenty men escaped in three small boats. All they could see around them was an endless, empty ocean. For the next three months, they were blown across the stormy Pacific. The men on one of the boats became so hungry that they did something terrible. The youngest sailor was shot by his crewmates—and then eaten!

▼ This painting of a whale sinking the *Essex* is part of a 1,246-foot- (380-m-) long painting made in the 1840s.

TALE OF A WHALE

Herman Melville told the story of the *Essex* again in his story *Moby Dick*. The novel is about Captain Ahab's search to find Moby Dick, the white whale that bit off his leg. Melville had been a whale-hunter and knew of a real whale, Mocha Dick, that may have killed about 30 men.

ARCTIC MYSTERY

Two ships, *Erebus* and *Terror*, sailed from Britain in May 1845. The ships were built with iron, to be extra strong, and they were driven by train engines. Sir John Franklin was their commander, or man in charge. He was a famous explorer, and he was hoping to sail through the thick ice of the Arctic.

◄▼ A picture of Sir John Franklin, who was shipwrecked on the ships *Erebus* and *Terror*, shown below.

The ships were last seen on July 26, 1845, tied up beside a huge iceberg north of Canada. Over the next 14 years, 40 rescue parties set out to search for the missing ships. But the *Erebus* and *Terror* had disappeared.

The mystery was finally solved when the Inuits, an Arctic people, showed explorers a pile of rocks. Buried inside was a tin box that held Franklin's last report. For three terrible winters, the *Erebus* and *Terror* had been stuck in the ice of the frozen seas. The report was written the day before the crews left their helpless ships and tried to walk to safety. As a trail of bones showed, not one of them had survived.

▲ *Erebus* and *Terror* sail past the icebergs of the Arctic.

GHOSTSHIPS

For many years, Arctic travelers kept finding things from Franklin's journey, such as slippers, spoons, a skeleton with a gold tooth, and a silver watch. But the wrecks of the *Erebus* and *Terror* have never been found. They may still be held in floating ice, that carries them like ghostships across the Arctic.

THE VANISHED CREW

On December 4, 1872, the ship *Dei Gratia* was sailing 621 miles (1,000 km) from the coast of Portugal. Suddenly the crew noticed a strange ship drifting past. Its sails were torn and ripped, and nobody seemed to be on board. On its side was written the name, *Mary Celeste*.

▲ Captain Benjamin Briggs was in charge of the *Mary Celeste* when she disappeared.

▶ The crew of the *Mary Celeste* seemed to have left the ship in a hurry.

The captain of the *Dei Gratia* sent two sailors to look at the ghostly ship. Nobody was on board. Water lay in the cabins, but the ship was in no danger of sinking. The ship's lifeboat was missing, but the crew's belongings were still there. What had caused them to leave the ship?

A DETECTIVE STORY

A story published in 1883 was said to have been written by someone who had been on the *Mary Celeste*. It said that one of the crew had murdered the others. Many people believed the story, but it was made up by Sir Arthur Conan Doyle. He was the man who wrote about detective Sherlock Holmes!

◄ Sailors from the *Dei Gratia* row towards the silent, empty *Mary Celeste*.

The *Mary Celeste* had sailed from New York a month before, carrying 1,700 barrels of alcohol. People have come up with many ideas about why the ship's crew disappeared. Some said it was an attack by pirates or even a giant squid! Perhaps the huge amount of alcohol on board caused an explosion. This scared the crew, who escaped in the lifeboat. Storms then flooded the *Mary Celeste*, but she sailed silently on while her crew's little lifeboat sank beneath the waves.

THE TITANIC

► A painting of the *Titanic* hitting an iceberg.

Captain Smith of the *Titanic* had received several warnings about icebergs that day, but he had not slowed his ship down. When the sailor on lookout saw the mountain of ice coming out of the darkness, he quickly rang a bell. But it was too late.

A TITANIC DEPTH

The *Titanic* sank to the bottom of the Atlantic to an amazing depth of over 2.5 miles (4 m). It was impossible for people to dive to such depths in the past. But in 1985 the shipwreck was found with the help of a modern submarine that could dive deep enough to find the wreck. Millions watched pictures of the wrecked *Titanic* 73 years after it had sunk.

The ship turned too slowly to miss the danger, and just before midnight on April 14, 1912, an iceberg cut a hole in the *Titanic*'s side. One passenger said that the crash felt like a giant finger scratching the ship. This last desperate message was sent by radio telegraph, "SOS. We have struck iceberg. Sinking fast."

The *Titanic* was traveling from Southampton, England, to New York City on its first voyage. This was the largest, most expensive liner ever built. People said that it could never sink, and because of this there was only enough space in the lifeboats for a third of the passengers.

Another ship, the *Californian*, lay only 18.5 miles (30 km) away. Why it didn't come to help when rockets were fired from the sinking ship is still a mystery. Less than three hours after the iceberg hit, the *Titanic* tipped up slowly and sank into the Atlantic. Over 1,500 people died in the freezing seas.

▲ This amazing photograph, taken in 1985, shows the wreck of the *Titanic* on the seabed.

▼ These people were among the lucky survivors who rowed to safety in the *Titanic*'s lifeboats.

VICTIM OF WAR

The cruise ship the *Lusitania* was heading toward the British coast on May 7, 1915. Britain was at war with Germany, so any ship near Britain might be attacked by German submarines. But the *Lusitania* was full of people on vacation, including many from the United States, which was not at war. Surely, nobody would dare to sink it.

◄ This medal was made so that people would remember the sinking of the *Lusitania*.

Suddenly a torpedo crashed into the ship's side with a huge bang. Normally, a ship takes hours to sink. But the *Lusitania* was hiding special cargo. She carried a secret load of weapons, including explosives. The torpedo set off a huge explosion, and the *Lusitania* sank in only 18 minutes, killing 1,195 people. The front of the ship hit the ocean floor while her back end still stuck out of the water.

► This poster was made to show people that they could travel between England and the United States on the *Lusitania*.

People were very angry about the sinking of the *Lusitania* by the Germans. Britain made thousands of posters of the ship to make British men want to join the army. People in the United States were very angry about the loss of 124 American lives on the ship. Two years later, the United States joined the war against Germany.

▼ A German artist painted this picture of the *Lusitania* sinking.

MISSING TREASURE

People said that the *Lusitania* was carrying millions of pounds worth of gold and expensive paintings. Many divers have tried to find this treasure. They have dug up silver-plated spoons, gold watches, and brass clocks. But the mystery of the missing gold and paintings is still unsolved.

SHIPWRECK FACTS

Here's a selection of interesting facts and figures about shipwrecks.

Bell bottom
A diving bell was used to look around the bottom of the sea as long as 2,500 years ago by the ancient Greek writer Aristotle. He made many studies of the underwater world.

Sailing east
The ship's compass, which is used to tell which direction a ship is traveling in, was invented in China, and is described in a Chinese book from A.D. 1060.

RAFT OF THE MEDUSA

In 1816, 159 of those who survived the shipwreck of the French ship *Medusa* tried to sail to safety on a huge raft. Only four of them lived, and some of the people left ate those who died! This is a famous painting of the raft.

Early warning
The earliest known lighthouse was the Pharos of Alexandria, built around 280 B.C. to prevent shipwrecks on the Egyptian coast. It was said that people could see its light as far as 30 miles (48 km) away.

Great balls of fire
When some cast-iron cannonballs from the *Mary Rose* were lifted from the water, they did not mix well with the fresh air. They exploded!

Real Robinson
Robinson Crusoe, the famous story of a shipwrecked sailor on a desert island, was written by Daniel Defoe in 1720. It was based on the life of a Scottish sailor named Alexander Selkirk.

Warning bell
When a ship that is insured by the famous company Lloyds of London is wrecked, the Lutine Bell is rung. This famous bell was saved from the wreck of the *Lutine* that sank in 1799 with a load of gold and silver bars.

SOS
The SOS sent by the *Titanic*'s radio was one of the first uses of this call for help. Some people say it stands for "Save our souls." In fact SOS is the quickest signal that can be sent in an emergency. Before 1908, the code for a call for help was CQD. Some people said this meant "Come quick, danger."

WRECKING NATURE

When the oil tanker *Exxon Valdez* was wrecked on the coast of Alaska, the oil that it was carrying spilled out over 1,243 miles (2,000 km) of coastline and killed hundreds of thousands of animals.

▲ A lifeboat crew in 1910 pull their boat up on to the beach.

Lifesavers
After the *Titanic* sank, a new law was written which said that ships had to carry enough lifeboats to hold all of the passengers.

Buried treasure
In the last 50 years, billions of pounds of gold and jewels have been found in shipwrecks on the ocean floor. One wreck off Indonesia is thought to still hold treasure worth over $715,000,000.

Old wrecks
There are over 30,000 known shipwrecks around the coast of Britain. Although some shipwrecks are thousands of years old, it is only in the last 50 years that people have had the machines needed to look for them.

The U.S. Coast Guard
The U.S. Coast Guard has many duties. It rescues thousands of people from disasters. It saves property from shipwrecks and floods.

St. Nicholas
Better known as Santa Claus, St. Nicholas is also the saint who is believed to look after sailors. He is said to have saved the lives of his friends when they were shipwrecked off the coast of Turkey.

Here are some interesting facts about two old and two more recent shipwrecks.

Shipwreck	Size (tons)	Built	Sank	How many died?	How many saved?
Mary Rose	700	1511	1545	about 650	about 50
Vasa	1,300	1628	1628	about 50	about 150
Lusitania	30,396	1907	1915	1,195	764
Titanic	46,329	1911	1912	1,502	705

SHIPWRECK WORDS

▲ Shipwrecks can be full of treasure, like these gold coins from the *Douro* which sank in 1882.

This glossary explains some words used in this book that you might not have seen before.

archaeologists (ar-kee-OL-uh-jists) People who study history by looking at things such as old buildings, shipwrecks, or treasure.

Armada (ar-MAH-duh) A large group of warships, especially the Spanish ships sent to attack England in 1588.

barrel (BA-ruhl) A wooden container often used to hold liquids such as water, beer, or wine.

cargo (KAR-goh) The goods and materials being transported by a ship.

cradle (KRAY-duhl) A framework used to hold a shipwreck when it is being lifted or moved.

detectives (di-TEK-tivz) Policemen or other people who try to solve crimes and mysteries by looking for clues.

icebergs (EYESS-bergs) Huge masses of ice floating in the sea.

lifeboat (LIFE-boht) A small boat carried on a ship or launched from the shore to save lives at sea.

liner (LINE-uhr) A ship—part of a group of similar ships owned by the same company or "line."

lookout (LUK-out) Someone who sits and keeps watch from high on a ship.

mermaids (MUR-maydz) Imaginary sea creatures, with the head and body of a woman and the tail of a fish.

pirates (PYE-rits) Sailors who travel around the seas stealing from other ships.

reefs (reefs) Ridges of rock, sand, or coral in the sea, on which ships are often wrecked.

scarab (SCAR-uhb)
A jewel cut in the form of a beetle. Scarabs were very popular in ancient Egypt.

shipwreck (SHIP-rek)
This can describe the destruction or sinking of a ship at sea, and also the remains of that ship.

smugglers (SMUHG-lurz)
People who break the law by bringing items into a country without paying extra money to the government for them.

skeleton (SKEL-uh-tuhn)
The skeleton is the frame that the bones inside our bodies make. It supports our bodies.

SOS
A call for help that ships often use when they are in trouble.

▲ Hunting for whales was once a good way to make money—but also a very dangerous one!

survivors (sur-VYE-vurz)
People who are involved in a disaster such as a shipwreck but live to tell the story.

technology (tek-NOL-uh-jee)
The study of subjects like science and engineering.

torpedo (tor-PEE-doh)
A missile fired by a submarine.

trade
Trade is what happens when one person offers another person something in return for something else. This may be money or some other item.

whale hunting (HUHNT-ing)
There used to be many whale hunters. Thousands of whales were killed so that parts of their bodies could be used to make candles, perfume, and even clothing.

wireless radio telegraph (WIRE-lis RA-dee-oh TEL-uh-graf)
A radio used to send and receive messages.

wreck (REK)
This is what is left of something when it has been destroyed. The wreck of a boat might be pieces of wood, tools, and things that belonged to the sailors who had once lived on the ship.

◄ Mermaids were painted in pictures and carved on the *Vasa*'s wooden cabin walls.

SHIPWRECK PROJECTS

VISIT A SHIPWRECK

Lots of countries have an amazing history of warships and trading ships, shipbuilders and sailors, smugglers and shipwrecks. There have been thousands of wrecks around the world's coasts, and many of them are shown in local museums.

If you live near the ocean, or when you go to visit such an area, ask at the library or tourist information center if there is a ship museum near you. Try to find out the history of any local shipwrecks, lighthouses, and lifeboats.

DRAW A SHIPWRECK MAP

Find a map of the world in an atlas and copy it on to a large sheet of paper. Now use websites and books from the library to find out about as many shipwrecks as you can. Mark each shipwreck in the correct place on your map with a drawing of the ship. See if you can find photographs of the treasures from each wreck and stick them to your shipwreck map. Draw the illustrations if you cannot find pictures to cut out.

▲ These sailors' belongings, including a purse and a comb, were found on the *Mary Rose*.

SHIPWRECKS ON THE WEB

If you have access to the Internet, you may be able to track down information including photos of shipwrecks and their treasures. Some sites will also tell you about dives to shipwrecks that are happening at the moment. Here are a few websites to try:

▲ You can visit the *Mary Rose* in Portsmouth, England, or look up its website!

http://www.maryrose.org
Take a tour of the *Mary Rose* museum. This has a 3-D model of the *Mary Rose*. You can have your hair cut by the ship's barber-surgeon, visit the ship's cook in his galley and fire the cannons with the gunners.

http://blackbeard.eastnet.ecu.edu
Find out the latest news from dives that are going on to the shipwreck of the *Queen Anne's Revenge*. This is said to be the famous pirate Blackbeard's ship! The website is great fun, with shots fired at you from Blackbeard's ship, and a puzzle to put together the pirate's treasure.

http://www.vasamuseet.se
The home page of the *Vasa* Museum, with some great photographs.

http://ina.tamu.edu
Institute of Nautical Archaeology

An excellent site with thousands of photographs of shipwrecks and their treasures, including Ulu Burun, and maps of shipwreck sites.

You can search for other shipwreck sites using any search engine. Try using the search phrases "shipwrecks," "maritime," or just the name of a ship or shipwreck you want to find out about, such as the *Lusitania*.

CAPTAIN OF A SHIPWRECK

Imagine that you are the captain of a ship that is carrying a load of treasure to a foreign country. Suddenly a disaster hits your ship—a pirate attack, a bad storm, or whatever you decide. Write a story about how you try to save your ship and what happens. When you escape, do you try to save the treasure, and if so, what do you do with it? If you want to bury your treasure, you could draw a map of where it is hidden so that you can collect it later.

INDEX